LARGE FORCES

WHAT'S MISSING IN PUBLIC ADMINISTRATION

ALASDAIR ROBERTS

Revised June 2014

Copyright © 2014 Alasdair Roberts

"Good day, dear friend, where are you coming from?"

"From the Museum, where I have spent three hours. I saw everything they have there, and examined it all carefully. There were so many astonishing things, that I am neither strong enough nor clever enough to give you a full description of it all. What birds and beasts I saw there! What flies, butterflies, cockroaches, and beetles! And what tiny cochineal insects! Some of them are smaller than a pin's head."

"But did you see the elephant? And what did you think it looked like? You must have felt as if you were looking at a mountain."

"Are you quite sure it's there?"

"Quite sure."

"Well, brother, you mustn't be too hard upon me. To tell the truth, I didn't notice the elephant."

> Ivan Andreyevich Krylov (1769-1844),
> *The Fable of the Inquisitive Man*

CONTENTS

1	Our Neglect of Large Forces	1
2	The Myth of the Prewar Orthodoxy	5
3	The Mess We're In	21
4	Is APD Eating Your Lunch?	39
5	Why It Matters	48
	Notes	56

1

OUR NEGLECT OF LARGE FORCES

Government, Woodrow Wilson said in 1889, "does whatever experience permits or the times demand."[1] Wilson, the man we now hail as the father of American public administration,[2] sat in his office at Wesleyan University, and what he wrote was a sensible response to the changes he saw in the world around him.

In 1889 the United States was celebrating the centenary of the inauguration of President Washington. Washington would have been astonished by changes in the role and structure of the federal government over that century, had he lived to see them. The federal government had acquired and settled two million square miles of land, mustered and pensioned hundreds of thousands of soldiers, established a national banking system, and promoted the construction of a railroad network so vast that the track, if laid in a straight line, would circle the earth seven times. Now it was preparing to build a powerful steam navy and manage the entry of a half-million immigrants a year.

Of course, the execution of these tasks had not been easy, partly because it required the development of a bureaucracy that was, by the standards of that time, disturbingly large and expensive. But the truth of what Wilson said in 1889 could not be denied. Although the process of adaptation might have been painful and slow, and its path influenced by a host of institutional and cultural considerations peculiar to the United States, the federal government *had* changed in fundamental ways. Eventually, government did what the times demanded.

Many years later, in 1951, Henry A. Turner published an article in *The Western Political Quarterly* that explained how Wilson thought about the evolution of American government. Turner wrote that Wilson subscribed to "an organic theory of government [which held that] the United States had not developed according to conscious planning, but had evolved to its present form through custom, practice, the impact of dominant personalities, and social and political forces."[3]

Turner was a Missourian who had returned from wartime service in the North Atlantic to complete his PhD at the University of Chicago. He worked under the supervision of Leonard White, who was probably the most prominent scholar in American public administration at that time. In his 1951 article, Turner did not merely describe Wilson's way of thinking. He articulated a point of view that was shared by White and many other academics in public administration. This helps explain why so many scholars in the field identified Wilson as their intellectual forebear. Like Wilson, these scholars took a pragmatic view about the role and structure of government. They, too, had seen the country buffeted by powerful forces—such as the ebb and flow of global trade and finance, mass migrations, technological revolutions, and the competition of great powers. To them, it seemed impossible to fully understand the administrative apparatus of government without studying the large forces that had caused it to come into being. What government did, and how it did it, could not be explained without accounting for the pressure applied by those forces.

This basic proposition, so widely accepted in the 1930s and 1940s, has been largely forgotten by scholars in the field of public administration in the United States. Few give serious attention to the ways in which large forces affect the role and structure of government. Furthermore, the intellectual history of the field is often written as though no one had *ever* addressed that subject. Admittedly there are scholars in political science who claim an interest in the evolution of the administrative apparatus of government. They even credit some of the early pioneers in public administration, including Leonard White, for blazing the trail that they are now following. But their body of work is flawed, for reasons we will explore later. Moreover, it garners little attention in the field of public administration. Scholars in public administration abandoned this territory long ago, and have little interest in how others subsequently cultivated it.

The field of American public administration is weaker because of its neglect of large forces and their effects on the administrative apparatus of government. Certainly, scholars in the field do a great deal of important and rigorous research. But a disproportionate amount is concerned with narrow questions of administrative technique. We have lost the capacity to tell broader stories about the processes by which the administrative apparatus of government has acquired its present form. This is one reason why the public relevance of the field has diminished since the establishment of its main association, the American Society for Public Administration, in 1939. Big questions about the evolution of government are left to scholars from other fields, such as political science, economics, or history. Scholars in public administration cannot provide a coherent account of how government

LARGE FORCES

responded to the operation of large forces in the past, and as a result they are unable to provide useful advice on how the country should respond to the operation of those forces in the future. We are like the crew in a ship's lower decks. We might understand how its propulsion and navigation systems work, but we have no real sense of where the ship is sailing from, where it is heading, or why it follows one route rather than another.

2

THE MYTH OF THE PREWAR ORTHODOXY

Most prominent scholars in the field of American public administration in its early years shared an interest in the processes by which large forces influenced the role and structure of government. We do not recognize their interest in this subject today, because we are blinded by a widely accepted but inaccurate story about the intellectual history of the field.

Conventional wisdom about the early years of public administration says that it began with a phase of intellectual dogmatism that was not broken until the years immediately after World War II. Two scholars, Dwight Waldo and Herbert Simon, are credited with freeing the field from the ice sheet that is said to have immobilized it in the prewar years. It is acknowledged that Waldo and Simon had starkly different views about the direction the field should take once it had been liberated: Waldo wanted a greater emphasis on political theory, and Simon wanted more rigorous scientific inquiry. But they had inadvertently collaborated on collapsing the old dogma and launching the field of public administration into an age of intellectual pluralism.

This received wisdom about the origins of the field is wrong in two ways. The first is that the field of public administration did not suffer from a phase of intellectual dogmatism that lasted until the postwar years. The second is that Waldo and Simon did not lay out the only lines of attack against that dogma, such as it was. A more accurate view would recognize that the field was unsettled in the prewar years. Leading scholars understood that that their knowledge of the field was limited and unreliable. In particular, they knew that their ideas about public administration had been shaped by circumstances—and that as circumstances changed, so might their ideas. In short, the very individuals who are alleged to be the guardians of the prewar dogma had identified one of the main lines of attack against it, one not really emphasized by either Waldo or Simon. These alleged guardians of orthodoxy actually had a way of thinking about administration, shaped by a broad world view and hard experience, that recognized the contingent quality of their knowledge.

Wallace Sayre, a professor of political science at Columbia University, played an important role in propagating the idea that public administration had been intellectually ossified until the late 1940s.[4] In 1958 Sayre published an article in *Public Administration Review* claiming that theory in the field had been "codified" in the 1930s. There was a "prewar orthodoxy," Sayre said, which was articulated most powerfully in the 1937 report of the President's Committee on Administrative Management. Any further development in public administration theory was suspended during the war, Sayre argued. Only after the war was this orthodoxy challenged, during a period of "dissent and heterodoxy." Sayre recounted how Waldo, in his 1948 book *The Administrative State*, had "demonstrated how value-loaded, how culture-bound, how political—in short, how 'unscientific'—were the premises, the 'principles,' the logic, of orthodox public administration." Meanwhile Simon, in his 1947 book *Administrative Behavior*, had revealed the prewar orthodoxy to be a jumble of "proverbs" rather than the product of a true administrative science.[5]

Ironically, Sayre's argument about the rise and fall of the prewar orthodoxy has itself become a fixture of the intellectual history of public administration. It has survived more than fifty years, which makes it far more resilient than the prewar orthodoxy itself, had it actually existed.

A few minutes of reflection will show how unlikely it is that an orthodoxy could have existed at that time. Let us begin by taking the concept seriously. Orthodoxy is a term more commonly used to describe religious belief. It implies a condition in which certain ideas are unchallenged and unchallengeable. It suggests rigidity and closed-mindedness. When we say that the prewar leaders of public administration were engaged in the propagation of an orthodoxy, we are saying, in essence, that they had stopped thinking. We should ask whether this is a reasonable supposition given the conditions of that time. As Beryl A. Radin has recently observed, the world was in flux, and these were worldly, well-educated men and women, most of whom were deeply engaged in the practice of administration.[6] Would they have been certain that what they knew about the subject of administration was all they would ever need to know?

Consider the large forces that were at work in the United States in the thirteen years between the publication of Leonard White's *Introduction to the Study of Public Administration* (1926), generally recognized as the first textbook in the field, and the establishment of the American Society for Public Administration (1939):

— *Trade and finance.* The United States was part of a global system of trade and finance that was volatile and, because of its global reach, extraordinarily difficult to influence. The crash of 1929 and the depression of the 1930s were not unprecedented. Older scholars of public administration had already lived through the Panic of 1907, the deep recessions that preceded World War I, and the depression of 1920-21. Even before the crash of 1929, experts debated how the American economy could be induced to behave more consistently.

— *International relations.* Meanwhile, the order that had provided a degree of stability within international relations in the nineteenth century had broken down. The relative power of nations was changing, and competition among them was becoming more violent. The United States, itself an emerging great power, was deeply affected by these changes. It had already been pulled into World War I and spent a considerable part of the 1920s attempting to avoid a resurgence of conflict. The U.S. federal government was worrying about military preparedness well before the outbreak of war in Europe in 1939. The rise of the Japanese Empire also complicated plans to grant independence to the Philippines—a territory more populous than any state of the union, and still under federal control at the time of Franklin Roosevelt's election.

— *Technology.* The United States was in the midst of the most important technological shift in its history. There were four radical innovations: the automobile, the airplane, large-scale electricity generation and distribution, and radio broadcasting. All of them posed challenges for the federal government: regulating new enterprises; providing infrastructure such as roads and airports; and applying new technologies to national defense.

— *Demography.* The nation was also experiencing large-scale changes in the distribution and characteristics of its population. American cities grew by 75 percent between 1910 and 1940, while the rural population stagnated. Millions of African Americans migrated from southern to northern states between the two world wars, and there was a second great migration from midwestern to western states during the 1930s. These population shifts had direct implications for politics and administration at the federal level.

— *Disease.* At the same time, Americans struggled with major threats to public health. In January 1937—the very month that the president's committee released its report on federal reorganization—the United States was battling an influenza epidemic that, in some parts of the country, rivaled the pandemic of 1918–19. Roosevelt himself was the symbol of another disease whose rapid spread terrified the American public: polio. In 1934, California had called on the federal government for help in managing one of the worst polio epidemics in American history.

— *Climate.* And finally there was the problem of "climate change," a phrase that became familiar to Americans as drought afflicted the Great Plains during the 1930s. Rexford Tugwell, an adviser to Roosevelt, said that this episode of climate change posed "one of the most serious peacetime problems in the nation's history."[7] Federal officials struggled with a now-familiar set of questions: Had human activity caused the drought? Was the change temporary or permanent? And was it possible to adapt to the change, or should farmers simply abandon the land?

The leaders of the new field of public administration were acutely conscious of the breadth and scale of the forces that were pressing on American government, and they responded to their predicament just as we would expect reasonably intelligent people to do: not by laying down hard rules about administration, but by adopting a policy of experimentation and open-mindedness. This was certainly true of the three people that Wallace Sayre thought carried a particular responsibility for constructing a prewar orthodoxy. These were the members of the President's Committee on Administrative Management: Charles Merriam, Louis Brownlow, and Luther Gulick.

Merriam, a professor of political science at the University of Chicago, was in the final years of his academic career, a phase in which we might have expected him to evince some doctrinal inflexibility. But this was not the case. In 1926, Merriam had published a paper that cautioned explicitly against orthodoxy in research. "All architecture," he said, "need not be Gothic."[8] Six years later, in a book published shortly before the president's committee began its work, Merriam gave another warning against intellectual rigidity. He said that the world faced "fundamental changes in the political, the industrial, the religious, the scientific order, changes that will shatter many of the existing power structures beyond recognition," and that the future would belong to those who "grope their way forward from chance to choice, from blind adaptation to creative evolution."[9] The festchrift that was prepared for Merriam in 1941 showed that he remained a broad-minded scholar who was sensitive to the ways in which large forces were disrupting traditional attitudes about the role and organization of government.[10]

Of the three members of the president's committee, it is Luther Gulick who is usually singled out as the strongest champion of a prewar orthodoxy. In 1937, shortly after the publication of the committee's final report, Gulick collaborated on the publication of a volume that attempted to articulate scientifically based "principles of administration."[11] Often, this single publication is presented as evidence of Gulick's preference for simple and rigid doctrine.

In reality, like Merriam, Gulick was a pragmatist. He believed that the forms of administration were shaped by "experimentation and trial" in response to "the pressure of circumstances."[12] Toward the end of his career, Gulick said that the content of the field of public administration "is set by the environment, not by logic."[13] He had taken the same position at the time of Franklin Roosevelt's first inauguration decades earlier:

> The working arrangements of modern government are not so much the result of theory as of the process of trial and success. . . . But the process of change is slow. At the present moment, the government of the part of the world in which we live is in many respects three generations behind our necessities and our social and economic world. [14]

Gulick's true attitude was further illustrated in two books completed shortly after World War II. The first, published in 1948, drew on his experiences in wartime administration. Gulick began with a recounting of the war years that combined "the stream of military, political and economic events and . . . the stream of administrative events." He explained his rationale for interweaving these two narratives:

> It is important for our purposes to recognize these two interrelated streams because, before we are through, it is my hope that we will be able to add further evidence to substantiate the thesis that *administrative developments, like organic developments, cannot be understood unless they are related (1) to their own organic past and (2) to the compulsions of the environment in which they exist.*[15]

Gulick worked from the same premise in a study of American forest policy that he completed a short time later. He examined "the administrative problems . . . created for government" as it addressed the problem of timber depletion. The American system of forest administration, Gulick insisted, "emerged historically piece by piece."[16] And so historical inquiry was essential to understand why the system had evolved into its present form:

> When government . . . takes positive action to solve an economic problem, what happens? What is the chain of events that is set in motion? No one knows enough about economics or the political and social sciences to tell in advance what the chain reactions will be, or where the chain will end. It is possible, however, to trace these reactions historically in connection with the older and well-established governmental programs.[17]

In the *Journal of Politics*, the political scientist John Gaus praised Gulick for writing

> a type of study in which the roots and settings of government policy . . . are included in the appraisal of institutions, instruments, procedures and programs. . . . It is a type of political economy enriched and made more meaningful by an awareness of the influence of time and place, evolving culture, varieties of institutional and personal adaptations, and scientific research."[18]

We can begin to see that the early years of public administration were not captured by an orthodoxy. On the contrary, they were suffused with the sense that the administrative apparatus of government was constantly evolving in response to changes in the society in which it was embedded. Scholars of public administration also recognized that the process of adaptation was complicated and poorly understood.

John Gaus of the University of Wisconsin might have been the first academic to acknowledge this gap in understanding. In 1929 he was commissioned by the Social Science Research Council to conduct a survey of research in the new field. In 1931 he summarized his findings. The field, he said, was "handicapped by a lack ... of any sense of the historical continuity of administrative developments. Very little work has been done by the political scientist in reappraising our administrative history." Gaus had a clear idea of what the object of historical inquiry ought to be. The goal, he thought, should be to explain how the evolution of public administration in the United States had been influenced by factors such as industrialization, immigration, urbanization, war, and technological innovation.[19]

Gaus took his own advice to heart in his 1940 study of the United States Department of Agriculture, which explained its development as the result of "the forces present in ... American and world political economy."[20] In that book, Gaus also elaborated on his general approach: "Administrative problems have their roots in social and political forces," he said. The researcher's task was to "become an ecologist" who examines how these forces produce "alterations in organization and procedure" within government departments.[21]

Gaus expanded on this "ecological approach" in a lecture at the University of Alabama in 1945: "The study of public administration must begin with some explanation of why people burden themselves with something which many of them, at least, resent." The proper method of addressing this question, he said, was to consider how "environmental change is linked with public administration. . . . There is an explanation of the functions of government in the changes which take place in its environment, changes which coerce us into the use of government as an instrument of public housekeeping and adjustment." He listed factors that were most important in explaining the evolution of governmental functions:

> They are: people, place, physical technology, social technology, wishes and ideas, catastrophe, and personality. I have over many years built up a kind of flexible textbook in a collection of clippings, articles and books illustrative of each, as anyone can do for himself. . . . [This is] the raw material of a science of administration . . . which describes and interprets why particular activities are undertaken through government and the problems of policy, organization and management generally that result from such origins.

In his Alabama lecture, Gaus noted a few of the "environmental factors" that had influenced public administration over the preceding decades, or seemed likely to influence it in the future: the shift of population from farms to cities, the advent of the automobile and the atomic bomb, the obsolescence of older forms of transport, and the rise of modern industry and a world economy.[22]

Gaus, nearing the end of his career, did not vigorously follow this line of inquiry. But he made clear in later writing that he still considered the study of "environmental, population and technological change" to be a matter of fundamental importance in public administration. Administrative technique could not be divorced from context. Personnel classification, for example, was not merely a matter of applying abstract administrative principles to bureaucratic practice. The subject, he said in 1951, "raises questions of the nature of the changing functions of government . . . that go deep into the adjustment of people to their environment."[23]

Gaus was not alone in believing that scholars had to address the question of how environmental factors shaped administration. In the early 1930s, for example, Earle Ross of Iowa State College published a study that explained how "social forces" had shaped federal agricultural policy in the late nineteenth century.[24] Gaus considered it to be "a model of interpretation of administrative history."[25] In 1940, Fritz Morstein Marx edited a volume on public administration that included chapters on "the contextual or environmental conditions affecting the public service."[26] And the following year, Schuyler Wallace of Columbia University published a book that warned against studying administration in federal agencies without "broad consideration of the economic, social, and psychological characteristics of the society in which they are operating."[27]

In 1942, the recently established *Public Administration Review* published an appreciation of Tocqueville by Louis Smith, in which Smith praised Tocqueville's attention to the effects of "powerful forces" such as industrialization, recurrent economic crises, and war on the shape of American public administration.[28] This was followed by two articles in the same journal by Lynton Caldwell, published in 1943 and 1944, that examined how the ideas of Jefferson and Hamilton had been adapted to accommodate "the radically changing circumstances of American life."[29] Caldwell thought that this sort of historical analysis was essential to a proper understanding of American administrative theory and practice. "To understand an administrative system," he later explained, "requires an awareness of the ever-changing, interrelating forces and factors comprising its environment and shaping its existence."[30]

Observe that many of these works were published during the war years—the very period that Wallace Sayre would later characterize as dead years for public administration research. But they were not dead at all. Smith and Caldwell were not the only scholars who used the wartime pages of *Public Administration Review* to argue for a broad view of the new field. The idea that there was a close relation between administrative techniques and "social and political environment" (David Levitan, 1943), or the "social, geographic, and political environment"

(Donald Price, 1944), or "economic and social imperatives" (Vincent Barnett Jr., 1944) was routinely acknowledged in the journal's early years.[31] Administrative principles "are entirely relative," J. Donald Kingsley insisted in 1945:

> We need . . . to escape from the sterile conception that administration is an end itself. . . . This can best be done by the acquisition of perspective and by the careful analysis of administrative devices and techniques in relation to the broad ends they are to serve. . . . It follows that our approach to the discovery of administrative principles must be historical.[32]

Robert Dahl, writing in *Public Administration Review* in 1947, concurred. The study of public administration, he concluded, should be "a broadly based discipline, resting not on a narrowly defined knowledge of techniques and processes, but rather extending to the varying historical, sociological, economic, and other conditioning factors that give public administration its peculiar stamp in each country." Like Kingsley, Dahl doubted that there could be "*any* principles [of public administration] independent of their special environment."[33]

Leonard White, the first editor of *Public Administration Review*, deserves credit for giving several of these authors the opportunity to make the case for this broad approach to research. In some instances, he did more than provide an opportunity to publish: as a dissertation adviser to both Smith and Caldwell, he actively encouraged them to take this approach. At first glance, White might seem like an unlikely champion of this point of view. Sayre claimed that White's textbook, *Introduction to the Study of Public Administration*, played an important role in consolidating the prewar orthodoxy. In addition, White was closely tied to the three members the President's Committee on Administrative Management, which Sayre regarded as another vehicle for the propagation of orthodoxy. Even today, White is sometimes remembered as a champion of narrow-minded managerialism.[34]

But White's view of public administration was never so limited. Writing in 1933 in the *Encyclopedia of Social Sciences,* White observed that "the general character of administration has always been governed" by social, cultural, and technological considerations.[35] The 1926 edition of his textbook also emphasized the importance of understanding American public administration as a product of "the industrial revolution and its many social, economic, and political implications." In the 1939 and 1948 editions of the textbook, White added technological advances and "the catastrophic forces of depression and war" as critical determinants of the "form and spirit of public administration in the United States."[36] White warned in the 1948 edition that attempts to reduce knowledge of public administration to "propositions of universal validity" might fail because problems of administration were never purely technical. The best solution to a problem of administration, White said, varied according to context and experience.[37]

We can see that White was echoing a view that was widely held in the field of public administration at the time. Herbert Simon's 1947 critique of the field was barely off the press, and Dwight Waldo's 1948 critique was not yet on it. But neither book was necessary to destroy the supposed orthodoxy of the 1930s. Scarcely anyone believed that the principles of administration that had been articulated in the preceding twenty years should be taken as immutable truths. On the contrary, it was generally accepted that forms of administration were shaped by "powerful forces" (Louis Smith's phrase) or "environmental factors" (Gaus's phrase), and that these forces or factors were constantly changing. By this way of thinking, the world never stood still long enough for an orthodoxy to become established.

Well before Simon or Waldo had published their books, White had committed himself to a large project that was intended to illustrate how "the general character of administration" in federal government had developed over the preceding one hundred and fifty years. The political scientist Harvey C. Mansfield eventually hailed it as a "monumental study of the administrative evolution of our national government."[38]   Its first product was *The Federalists: A Study in Administrative History*, spanning the years 1789 to 1801, published by the Macmillan Company in May 1948. A second volume, *The Jeffersonians*, covering 1801 to 1829, was published scarcely three years later. It was "an excellent book," according to the *New York Times*.[39] Next came *The Jacksonians*, after another three-year pause: "fresh and stimulating," said the *Times*.[40]   *The Jacksonians* won the Bancroft Prize for American History in 1955. The fourth volume, *The Republican Era*, covering 1869 to 1901, was published in 1958 and won the Pulitzer Prize for history. White had planned a fifth volume, covering the Progressive Era and the New Deal, but he died from cancer shortly before the publication of *The Republican Era*.[41]

The line of argument that White pursued in these volumes will now be familiar to us.[42] The object of his attention was the "administrative system" of the federal government.[43] The central premise was that changes in the administrative system were predominantly dictated by large problems that the nation's leaders could not avoid, and which they struggled to manage, such as the challenges created by great power rivalries, territorial insecurity, the demands of an emerging economy, and the advent of steam power. In White's history, political ideals were often bent or abandoned as the nation's leaders struggled to manage such problems. Even the most talented politicians found themselves "frustrated by circumstances" and "coerced by events."[44] What really mattered, White said in *The Jacksonians*, was the "force of events." The development of the federal administrative system, White argued in that volume, was mainly explicable as "the result of changes in magnitude, in complexity, and in the influence of external forces."[45]

Many other scholars in public administration understood that White was experimenting with a mode of research that was novel and important. As Yale University's David Potter said in 1952, there was no "ready-made term" for what White was doing, "just as there were no ready-made models" for how to do it.[46] Calling it administrative history was not entirely accurate, because it obscured the fact that White was presenting a specific argument about the way in which administrative systems developed. Charles Wiltse acknowledged in *Public Administration Review* that the series of books "underline in fact a relationship between administration and basic constitutional, political and economic issues which makes it impossible to understand the one without adequate knowledge of the other."[47] Writing in *Public Administration Review* in 1948, John Gaus agreed that White's project had "general significance" beyond its immediate subject matter.[48] "It is difficult to measure the magnitude of his achievement," said Princeton University's Lucius Wilmerding Jr. "Mr. White's work . . . is bound to give an impetus to further studies."[49]

Unfortunately Wilmerding's forecast proved to be badly off the mark. Only a handful of scholars, most of them taught by White himself, applied his methods seriously. One of these scholars was Henry A. Turner, who published articles about Woodrow Wilson in the early 1950s. Another was Paul Van Riper, whose *History of the United States Civil Service* was published in 1958. Van Riper described his book as "the story of one administrative system as it developed over time, as it responded to various political and social pressures."[50]

Perhaps the most persistent of White's students was a Canadian, J. E. Hodgetts, whose 1955 book, *Pioneer Public*

Service, closely followed White's model.⁵¹ Hodgetts's book examined the evolution of the "administrative machine" in Canada during the nineteenth century. Its thesis was that Canada's public service "has been shaped by the environment in which it has had to operate and that changes in the environment bring about alterations in the public service."⁵² In the *American Political Science Review*, Gaus praised Hodgetts's book and hoped that he would "extend his account down into the present century and continue to relate a changing environment to the evolution of the public services. Political theory and political action alike need this approach."⁵³ Hodgetts followed Gaus's advice, producing a 1973 book, the *Canadian Public Service*, which brought his argument about the influence of "great environmental factors" on Canadian government into the twentieth century.⁵⁴ It was an impressive work. But it might also have been the last attempt within the field of North American public administration to provide a substantial account of the ways in which large forces influenced the development of administrative systems.

3

THE MESS WE'RE IN

Going forward, it will be helpful to have a phrase that refers to the mode of reasoning that I have argued was commonplace within the field of public administration until the mid-1950s. I call it *large forces reasoning*. By this I mean a way of thinking about public administration that recognized that the overall structure of the administrative system, and also the techniques of administration, were shaped by the operation of a certain set of large forces, which I have identified in the preceding chapter. John Gaus's ecological approach to public administration is one of the most coherent examples of large forces reasoning, but as we have seen there were many other scholars who thought about public administration in similar ways. One of the implications of this mode of reasoning is that anything we know about public administration is contingent on the existence of a certain state of affairs. As Robert Dahl said in 1947, we cannot really understand techniques and processes of administration unless we also understand the larger conditioning factors that brought them into being.

LARGE FORCES

My aim in this chapter is to illustrate how this mode of reasoning has been erased from generally accepted doctrine in the field of public administration. I do this by examining three books that are widely acknowledged to be important within the field today. A review of these books will illustrate the thoroughness with which this purging has been completed. It is not as though today's scholars have studied earlier works, weighed the merits of large forces reasoning, and explained why they have put it aside. The purging goes deeper than that. Some of today's key texts do not recognize that anyone ever thought this way. But there is also a paradox that is evident in these books. Despite the elimination of large forces reasoning from generally accepted doctrine, there are signs of recognition by editors and authors that something like it is essential to help students and practitioners to make sense of the field.

We will start with *The Public Administration Theory Primer*, by H. George Frederickson, Kevin B. Smith, Christopher W. Larimer, and Michael J. Licari.[55] The *Primer* describes itself as "a standard reference and text" in American public administration, which has been "adopted by scores of instructors [and] cited in hundreds of scholarly articles." The book, according to the authors, has provided "a comprehensive survey of the field for thousands of students and academics."[56]

One of the first observations that we can make about the *Primer* is how thoroughly it absorbed Wallace Sayre's interpretation of the early years of public administration. The prewar orthodoxy is mentioned dozens of times throughout the book. Luther Gulick is presented as someone who "embraced the orthodoxy." This "golden age of theoretical hegemony" is said to have persisted until it was dealt "mortal blows" by Dwight Waldo and Herbert Simon. They were "the two giants of the field at the time," and their work "defined the two dominant scholarly perspectives in the field for the next fifty years."[57]

As an exercise in the writing of intellectual history, the *Primer*'s treatment of the prewar orthodoxy is problematic. It is taken as a hard and indisputable fact. The possibility that this interpretation of the prewar period is contestable—that it is *merely an interpretation* of intellectual tendencies—is never contemplated. There is, therefore, no effort to explain how the notion was invented. Wallace Sayre's influential 1958 article about the prewar orthodoxy is never mentioned.

Of course there was no such orthodoxy, and Gulick never embraced it. As we have seen, there is more evidence to suggest that Gulick was actually an advocate of large forces reasoning. More generally, there was already intellectual ferment in the field in the postwar years, and it did not require the intervention of Waldo and Simon to generate it. Moreover, Waldo and Simon were not "the two giants of the field at the time." Their 1947-48 books were reworkings of their doctoral dissertations. If anyone was a giant of the field in 1947-48, it was Leonard White, author of the leading textbook in the field, the first editor of *Public Administration Review*, president of the American Political Science Association, the chair of Simon's dissertation committee, and an ardent proponent of large forces reasoning.

White is mentioned only once in the *Primer*, in a passing reference to his interest in the management of public works. There are no other facts about his life or work. His massive four-volume study is overlooked. Nor is there any mention of John Gaus's proposed ecological approach, or of Gulick's views on the need to attend to the "compulsions of the environment," or Robert Dahl's call for research on conditioning factors, or Lynton Caldwell's admonition about the importance of "the ever-changing, interrelating forces and factors" that shape administrative systems. All of this is omitted.

The *Primer* describes what the authors considered to be the central preoccupations of the field of public administration. The field is said to be concerned with "the substance of public organization behavior, public management, and public policy implementation."[58] Accordingly, the book examines subjects such as the control of bureaucracy, the behavior of bureaucrats and bureaucracies, modes of decision making within public bodies, and the design of structures for delivery of public services.

There are two notable gaps in the *Primer*'s overview of theory in public administration. Look again at the list of subjects with which the field is said to be concerned. There is no reference to the substantive functions that are actually performed by government. Why does government acquire responsibility for a particular task at a certain moment of time, and why are tasks abandoned later? Why are tasks distributed among levels of government in a particular way? Why does an administrative system grow in one period and shrink in another? None of these questions is addressed directly, because they are not considered to be central questions for the field.

Indeed, one of the distinctive features of the *Primer* is its inattention to the tasks actually performed by American governments over the last sixty years. A reader would not know that this was the era in which the United States became a superpower and built a massive military-industrial complex; that it developed a sophisticated domestic security apparatus; that it designed and abandoned different systems for managing the domestic and international economy; that it constructed an expansive system of highways and airports; that it became more active in environmental protection; or that it expanded educational systems and became more aggressive in enforcing civil rights. None of this is mentioned because it is not considered to be relevant to the task of theory-building. According to the *Primer*, there is no sense in which this sort of knowledge could improve the usefulness of theory—that is, it there is no way it could "increase our general understanding of public administration, and/or . . . improve the applied practice of public administration."[59]

A second gap in the *Primer*'s overview of theory has to do with the set of variables that are thought to be relevant for exploring the subjects that are identified as central to the field. There is no systematic reference to any of the large forces that we listed earlier: international rivalries, economic transformations, technological advances, shifts in the pattern of disease, and demographic and climatic changes. A defender of the *Primer* might say that these forces are relevant in explaining *what* government does, and that this is not (as we have already observed) a main concern of the field. The *Primer*, they might argue, is more concerned with *how* government does its work: "the substance of public organization behavior, public management, and public policy implementation."

But are we so sure that an understanding of technique can be achieved without appreciation of these large forces? Few people in the so-called golden age of theoretical hegemony thought so. On the contrary, they rejected the "sterile conception" (J. Donald Kingsley's phrase from 1945) that administrative techniques could be understood without attention to the broader context in which they were applied. And a moment's reflection shows how this is true. For example, how can we understand recent changes in the structure of administrative systems without acknowledging our preoccupation with terrorist threats, or the information technology revolution, or shifts in the age structure and ethnic composition of the population?

Oddly, the *Primer* begins by criticizing a certain approach to theory-building in public administration and ends by reproducing the most-criticized features of that approach. The prewar orthodoxy is assaulted because it advanced its claims as the product of science without adhering to essential requirements of the scientific method, such as consciousness of fallibility and sensitivity to premises and contingencies. And yet the *Primer* separates theory-building from the realities of administration even more sharply. Luther Gulick and other supposed advocates of the orthodoxy never thought that it was possible to develop a theory of administration without also understanding what government actually does and the broader forces that shape its work. The *Primer*, by contrast, assumes that it is possible to do so. Moreover, it does not seem to recognize that it is making this assumption.

For further evidence of the extent to which large forces reasoning has been erased from the field of public administration, turn to *Classics of Public Administration*, edited by Jay M. Shafritz and Albert C. Hyde, which appeared in its seventh edition in 2012. We look at this book because it is regarded as one of the central texts in the field, like the *Primer*. The publisher of *Classics* promotes the volume as "part of the public administration DNA."[60] It is widely used as the main text in courses that address "fundamental concepts" or "intellectual history" in the field.

Classics is constructed as an anthology of "the most significant writings in the field."[61] The writings that are included in *Classics* tell a now-familiar story. The editors explain that the 1920s and 1930s were "a period of orthodoxy" in public administration. Thus there is an excerpt from Luther Gulick's 1937 paper, which is a "definitive statement" of the orthodox ideology. Later is a selection by Herbert Simon, who "refuted" the orthodox approach, and also one by Dwight Waldo, who bolstered Simon's assault on the orthodoxy, although with a different line of attack.[62]

Admittedly, there is a flicker of attention to large forces reasoning in *Classics*. There is an excerpt from Leonard White's 1926 textbook, and a passing observation by the editors that White took a "decidedly macro" approach to the study of public administration. And the excerpt itself clearly conveys White's view that the "concept of public administration" that was emerging at that time was driven by changes in the "social and economic environment." But this is as far as *Classics* goes, insofar as the selection of writings is concerned. There are no other works from the era that follow this mode of reasoning. The editors also provide a topical guide to writings, and none of the topics that are enumerated have anything to do with the large forces that concerned White and his contemporaries.[63]

Classics is flawed because of the procedure used to select the writings contained within it. The editors provide three criteria for the inclusion of works in the book. The first is that a selection "had to be relevant to a main theme of public administration . . . a basic statement that was consistently echoed or attacked in subsequent years." The second criterion is significance: "The selection had to be generally recognized as a significant contribution to the realm and discipline of public administration." And the third criterion is readability.[64]

Observe that the editors do not claim that the collection conforms to a fourth criterion, which is *representativeness*. There is no argument that the selections accurately convey the main intellectual trends within public administration at a particular moment of time. Relevance and significance are retrospective criteria: they judge the worth of a work based on what we think of it today. If an idea was dominant at a particular period, but was not "echoed or attacked" later, it is not relevant; and if its worth was not "generally recognized" later, it is not significant. The idea simply slips into oblivion, as though it had never been expressed at all. And that is what has happened to the many works that articulated some form of large forces reasoning.

The fact that *Classics* does not provide a representative overview of what people were actually thinking at a particular moment of time is not always appreciated by the editors. They say that the collection will give readers "a sense of the continuity of the discipline's thinking and show how the various writers and themes literally build on each other."[65] But the sense of continuity is an illusion. It is an artifact of the selection process. If we begin with the premise that selections should be guided by modern-day judgments of relevance and significance, then of course we will find a substantial amount of continuity. All the intellectual false starts and discordant notes have been erased from history, because they are no longer "echoed" or "recognized." It is like studying evolution without acknowledging any of the variations of species that became extinct along the way.

This confusion is not limited to the editors of *Classics*. Many teachers of courses that rely on the book are similarly misguided. One syllabus tells us that its aim is provide "an in-depth examination and analysis of the historical development of the field of public administration." Another says that its aim is to survey "the intellectual history of public administration, including the ideas, theories, practices, and debates fundamental to the evolution of the field from its inception to the present." But *Classics* cannot serve these purposes properly, because it makes no pretense of conveying history from the point of view of those who lived it. It describes only that part of the field's history that bolsters our present-day conceptions of what the field is about.

There is, however, an irony within the pages of *Classics*. Throughout the book, the editors provide brief passages that describe the "historical context" in which writings were produced. For example, the editors say that "the demands of industrial expansion" may have motivated the establishment of a merit-based civil service in the late nineteenth century. Later, they explain that alterations in the "size, scope, and reach of government" between 1910 and 1950 were driven by war, urbanization, and economic collapse. They say that the 1960s and 1970s were also a period of "dynamic change . . . politically, economically, and socially," while the 1980s and 1990s were shaped by "a remarkable string of political and economic events." And a "new era" in public administration is predicted in the new millennium because of "the pace and scale of political, economic, social and technological change in the environment."[66]

Of course, we recognize what the editors are doing in these passages: they are engaging in large forces reasoning. The editors are doing this because they are responsive to the needs of their readers. They know that readers must have this sort of analysis to make sense of the texts, and more broadly to understand the field that they are entering. Readers want to know why the shape of government has changed in the past, and how it is likely to change in the future. By engaging in this sort of analysis, the editors are unwittingly following in the footsteps of people like Leonard White and John Gaus (and even Luther Gulick). But all of this analysis is done informally, and in a sense illicitly. Scholars in public administration are not supposed to examine these big questions, and they are not supposed to employ large forces reasoning. The writings that have been selected for *Classics* make these proscriptions clear.

The editors of *Classics* wrestle with a conflict between the commitments of contemporary scholars in public administration (who generally ignore big questions and large forces) and the demands of students of public administration (who are clearly interested in big questions and large forces). They are not alone in this predicament. Widely used textbooks suffer from the same tension.

Consider, for example, *Public Administration: Understanding Management, Politics, and Law in the Public Sector*, by David Rosenbloom, Robert Kravchuk, and Richard Clerkin, which appeared in its seventh edition in 2009.[67] *Public Administration* is widely used as a textbook in introductory courses. It has several major competitors. Among them it has been lauded for giving "prominent attention to the development of the American administrative state."[68] Even so, *Public Administration* does not escape the conundrum that confronted the editors of *Classics*. The book itself tacitly concedes that the development of administrative systems is not recognized as a legitimate subject of inquiry within the field. Consequently any such analysis must be done hurriedly and loosely.

In their first chapter, the authors "establish the general boundaries and convey the major concerns of the discipline and practice of administration." They explain that public administration is concerned with the use of "theories and processes to fulfill legislative, executive and judicial mandates for the provision of governmental regulatory and service functions." And they report that "consideration of the leading definitions of public administration reveals that there are three distinct underlying approaches to the field," which they call the managerial, political, and legal perspectives.[69] The first emphasizes efficiency in operations; the second, popular control of operations; and the third, respect for the rule of law. These three perspectives are supposed to provide the framework for the whole of the 580-page book. Thus the topic of how public organizations should be structured is viewed from only the managerial, political, and legal viewpoints. So are the topics of how major decisions are taken, budgets are formulated, and workers are managed.

Observe that the inventory of approaches does not include any explicit form of large forces reasoning. That is, none the three approaches purport to explain the emergence and organization of governmental functions as a response to broader social forces, however that set of broader social forces might be defined. There is no "historical approach," as Leonard White might have called it; no "ecological approach," as John Gaus might have; and no "organic approach," as Luther Gulick might have. The authors do not directly deny the possibility that a fourth approach of this kind might be taken, but they strongly imply that no such approach is currently recognized within the field. Recall that the three approaches that *are* acknowledged—managerial, political, and legal—have been derived by canvassing the "leading definitions of public administration." Soon after, the authors say, with some degree of finality: "Public administration embodies three relatively distinct approaches that grow out of different perspectives on its functions." A little later, they add: "Once we have presented the gist of these three broad approaches, we will have completed our definitional discussion."[70]

The predicament confronting the authors becomes obvious in the second chapter of *Public Administration*, which seeks, among other things, to identify the causes of administrative growth.[71] Why do the authors bother with this topic? Probably because they, like their readers, recognize that it is difficult to make sense of the field without some understanding of how the administrative apparatus of government acquired its modern scale and design. But turn back to the preceding chapter, which defined "the general boundaries and . . . major concerns of the discipline and practice of administration."[72] Nowhere in *that* chapter is there any reference to the causes of administrative growth. The authors' definition of the field—which focuses more narrowly on the fulfilment of mandates for the provision of regulatory and service functions—does not naturally accommodate questions about the causes of growth. In this part of the second chapter, the authors have gone beyond the frontiers of the field in public administration, as they defined it in the first chapter.

The explanation of "the drivers of growth" that is provided in the second chapter is reproduced here:

> The primary drivers of administrative growth

and development have been associated with the increasing complexity of modern society, expanded public demands for public services, and the rise of the national defense establishment. In this vein, James Q. Wilson identified several roots of the development of the contemporary American administrative state. One was to provide a reliable postal service. The U.S. Post Office was not viewed as an end in itself but rather as a means of promoting economic development and national cohesion and integration. It was also spurred by a desire for political patronage. Wilson observes that "from 1816 to 1861, federal civilian employment in the executive branch increased nearly eightfold (from 4,837 to 36,672), but 86 percent of this growth was the result of additions to the postal service."

A second source of administrative growth has been the desire to promote economic development and social well-being through governmental action in various sectors of the economy. The Department of Agriculture was created in 1862, and the Departments of Commerce and Labor came into existence in 1913. More recently, the Department of Health, Education, and Welfare (now Health and Human Services) and the Departments of Housing and Urban Development, Transportation, Energy, and Education were created to promote governmental goals in these economic and social areas of American life. The Veterans Administration was made the Department of Veterans Affairs in the late 1980s. . . .

Another source of administrative growth has been defense. The Departments of War and

Navy were created in the 18th century, but the military establishment did not emerge as the federal government's largest administrative operation until after World War II. Since that time, the Department of Defense has often employed one-third or more of civilian federal workers. The Department of Veterans Affairs, functionally related to Defense, is also large (about 224,778 civilian employees). Interestingly, this means that more than 60 percent of federal civilian employees are employed in three agencies—Defense, Veterans Affairs, and the Postal Service. The creation of a standing army, navy, and air force and a large civilian administrative component to manage the military reflects the government's view that providing for the common defense requires centralized planning for the procurement and deployment of weapons and personnel.

In sum, the political roots of the development of contemporary public administration in the United States lie primarily in two political choices made by the government and society. First was that government would exist to promote such objectives as the common defense, economic development, and the general welfare. At the national level, this was a choice first made in the late 1780s and reinforced subsequently on many occasions. Second has been the choice, beginning in the 1880s or so, of placing heavy reliance on direct provision of services and functions by government as opposed to relying solely on the manipulation of subsidies for private action. As noted earlier, today the balance between steering and rowing is changing in conjunction with the NPM.[73]

Two observations can be made about this passage. First, it

is short, given its ambition. It proposes to describe the "primary drivers of administrative growth" over the course of two centuries within a few hundred words. And second, the analysis is rudimentary and in some respects flawed. For example, is the "rise of the defense establishment" really a *driver* of administrative growth? Or is it, instead, an example of growth—driven, perhaps, by the changing status of the United States within the international order? And once we put that aside, what other drivers are left? Principally the "desire to promote" goals such as economic development, national cohesion and integration, and social well-being. Choices are made—but in what context? There is hardly any mention of war, and no mention at all of economic calamities, migrations, or technological innovations. It is an explanation of administrative growth that appears to say little about the actual conditions in which government agencies were required to work.

However, this is not all that the authors have to say about the "drivers of administrative development." In fact, there are passing references to the subject throughout the text. Later, for example, we are told that the system of constitutional law is crucially important to American public administration, but that the law itself has adjusted throughout history to "continually changing political, economic, social, international, and environmental circumstances."[74] This is a different and more expansive set of "drivers" than were used in the second chapter, and it comes close to the set of environmental factors that would have been listed by scholars in the 1930s and 1940s. But the discussion is brief. We are warned that American public administration is built on shifting sand, and we are given an intimation of why the sand shifts, and that is the end of it.

Something similar happens in the book's discussion about the structure of public organizations. We are told that organizations will die if they fail to keep up with "the constantly changing technological, political, economic and social environments with which they must interact."[75] At first glance this seems like familiar language: Is it not also used to describe the forces that have shaped constitutional law? In fact, though, the list of factors has changed. Technology has been added and "international and environmental circumstances" have been eliminated. Why did the list change? We never find out. The subject is not explored further.

Environmental factors come up again when we discuss the subject of budgeting. The question from the second chapter reappears in a somewhat different form: "What causes growth in government expenditure?" The short answer is: "the same factors that gave rise to the administrative state (see Chapter 2)." Except that this is not quite right. Soon we are told that expenditure can be affected by "the interdependence of the United States and foreign economies, the rapidly changing character of international relations, and even the unpredictability of the weather's impact on agriculture and energy consumption." And further on we learn that new budget pressures will be created by the retirement of baby boomers. So here we have a set of factors affecting levels of expenditure—global economic interdependence, international relations, climate, and demography—that were not mentioned in the second chapter at all.[76]

The general problem in *Public Administration* is that it constantly engages in a form of large forces reasoning, but never does it consistently or in depth. Consider its discussion of public personnel administration. Why did the nation abandon the spoils system in the late nineteenth century? "Because its corrupt practices interfered with industrialization . . . [and harmed] international commerce."[77] Why did personnel practices become more draconian in the early 1950s? Because of anxieties provoked by the Cold War. Why did practices shift once again after the 1960s? Because of increased participation by women in the workforce, and then by the aging of the workforce. What is one of the main reasons why position classification schemes need constant maintenance? Because of rapidly changing technology. By the end of this discussion we have accumulated another list of environmental factors: industrialization, international politics, demographic change, and technological change. This is different than the list of drivers used in the second chapter, and not quite the same as any used in the discussions of budgeting, organizational design, and constitutional law.

Yet another list is compiled in the discussion of regulation. "The general origin of federal regulatory activities," we are told, "is associated with the tendency of industrialization to cause greater economic, technological, and social complexity of life during the past century or so."[78] The concept of industrialization is carrying a lot of weight here. It appears to encompass technological change, urbanization, and shifts in the structure of international finance. It even spans decades during which the country was engaged in the process of deindustrialization. But this expansively defined concept is still not big enough. Regulation, it turns out, it also driven by the empowerment of women and racial minorities. And also by "cultural changes [that] have increased our intolerance of risk."[79] Certainly, culture may be important—but why has it not been mentioned as a relevant consideration in the development of any other aspect of administration?

The difficulty that confronts the authors of *Public Administration* should now be clear. For commendable reasons, they want to engage in some mode of large forces reasoning. But their effort is complicated by the fact that the field itself does not recognize this as an appropriate mode of analysis. The approaches that are dominant within the field are not well suited to this form of analysis and provide no guidance on how it should be undertaken.

The result is that a form of large forces reasoning is employed, but it is not done explicitly or thoroughly. The book does not begin with a coherent enumeration of the forces that might affect different aspects of administration. The various concepts that are invoked (such as industrialization, international relations, and culture) are not defined. There is no consistent reference to the entire set of forces throughout the text. And there is no discussion of the mechanisms or processes by which administrative systems change in response to the operation of those large forces.

Over half a century, the field of public administration has painted itself into a corner. Through the decades, it has gradually expunged a certain body of work—made up of those writings that took large forces reasoning seriously—from its account of the field's intellectual history. Prevailing doctrine denies that the field has an interest in the subject of administrative development, or in the large forces that influence administrative goals and techniques. At the same time, however, there is a nagging sense that larger questions about administrative development must be addressed, especially for the purpose of orienting newcomers to the field, and that large forces are probably important for providing answers to those questions.

The educator Donald Schön once argued that professionals rely on two kinds of knowledge. One is espoused theory: the body of knowledge that a professional *says* he relies on. The other is theory-in-use: the body of tacit knowledge that the professional *actually* relies on.[80] Schön suggested that professionals are often unaware of the discrepancy between espoused theory and theory-in-use, and that this unawareness compromised their ability to learn. We might say the same about scholarship in public administration. There is a conflict between espoused theory, which ignores large forces reasoning, and theory-in-use, which sometimes recognizes its importance. But this conflict is never acknowledged, and as a result, theory-in-use is never improved.

4

IS APD EATING YOUR LUNCH?

In February 2013 W. W. Norton and Company published *Fear Itself: The New Deal and the Origins of Our Time* by Ira Katznelson, the Ruggles Professor of Political Science and History at Columbia University. It is a study of the New Deal years, which Katznelson says began with the inauguration of Franklin Roosevelt in 1933 and ended with the conclusion of the Truman presidency in January 1953. Katznelson examines how federal politics and administration were shaped by three events: the Great Depression, World War II, and the early Cold War. He emphasizes, more than earlier authors, the extent to which the design of the American welfare and warfare state was bent to accommodate the segregationist impulses of the American South. And he describes the way in which the migration of African Americans altered the politics of northern states, and eventually the character of federal policies as well.

Katznelson's book became a bestseller. *Kirkus Reviews*, one of the main guides for trade booksellers, called *Fear Itself* a "deeply erudite, beautifully written history" of the era,[81] while *Publishers Weekly* called it "a critical and deeply scholarly work that, notwithstanding, is compulsively readable."[82]

Few books in public administration published today receive such accolades, or a review of any sort in these outlets. In the last decade, *Kirkus Reviews* has published dozens of reviews that refer explicitly to political science—and none that refer to public administration. The same is almost true of *Publishers Weekly*. (There was one mention in 2005, in a review of a book written by Walden Bello, a professor of public administration at the University of the Philippines.) The situation is not much better with *Library Journal*, which is less concerned with the retail book trade. This journal has published two hundred and fifty reviews mentioning political science in the last decade, and fewer than ten mentioning public administration.

Of course, there was a time when public administration scholars wrote books that received comparable reviews. Leonard White received notices in *Publishers Weekly* for all four of the books in his administrative history of the United States, and also for winning the Bancroft and Pulitzer Prizes. Katznelson has actually recognized that *Fear Itself* is the sort of book that White might have liked to write. He celebrated its publication by delivering the Leonard D. White Memorial Lecture at the University of Chicago in April 2013, and began by acknowledging his debt to White's scholarship on "state making and public administration." Katznelson told his audience: "I identify, as some as you may know, with a subfield in American politics that puts itself under the rubric of American Political Development, and I have always thought of Leonard White . . . as the great-grandfather of APD."[83]

American Political Development (APD) is a subfield of the discipline of political science that came into its own in the 1980s. Karen Orren and Stephen Skowronek have described the subfield as one that is "guided by a theoretical precept . . . [that] because a polity in all its different parts is constructed historically, over time, the nature and prospects of any single part will best be understood within the long course of political formation."[84] Administrative systems are one of several aspects of political activity that capture the attention of APD scholars. And of course the premise is that administrative systems, like all other parts of the American polity, are "historically constructed."

Indeed, administrative systems are the main concern of *Building A New American State*, written by Stephen Skowronek and published in 1982. Today it is regarded as the "founding text of APD."[85] Skowronek's narrow aim was to examine three aspects of federal administration—the civil service, the army, and railroad regulation—between 1877 and 1920. But he also had a broader ambition, which was to develop a way of understanding the process of state-building more generally.

Skowronek appeared to subscribe to a form of large forces reasoning. He accepted the premise that "environmental imperatives" were an important cause of administrative development. (The environmental change that is most important in *Building a New American State* is industrialization.) But Skowronek rejected the idea that the process of administrative adaptation to changing conditions was straightforward. Administrative reform, he insisted, "was not simply a gradual accretion of appropriate governmental responses to environmental problems." Instead, the path of adaptation was determined by "political struggles rooted in and mediated by preestablished institutional arrangements."[86] A reviewer explained Skowronek's approach in these terms:

> Skowronek's underlying causal model is one in which the outcome of institution-building during any particular period of crisis is a function of both contemporaneous environmental factors, such as industrialization, and existing

institutional structures that are a product of past conditions.[87]

There is an echo here of Luther Gulick's 1948 thesis that "administrative developments . . . cannot be understood unless they are related (1) to their own organic past and (2) to the compulsions of the environment in which they exist."[88] Still, within the context of American political science in the late 1970s and 1980s, Skowronek's method was regarded as a novel and powerful way of explaining the development of the American state.[89]

Building a New American State was followed by other books that took a similar approach and which are now regarded as "canonic works" within APD.[90] In 1984, Richard Bensel published *Sectionalism and American Political Development*, which argued that the "development of government institutions" in the United States between 1880 and 1980 could not be understood without accounting for economic differences between the "advanced northern core and underdeveloped southern and western periphery."[91] Bensel followed this with his 1990 book, *Yankee Leviathan*, which examined the effect of "war and economy" on the development of the American state between 1859 and 1877, and in which Bensel asserted that the Civil War, and not the Revolutionary War, was the "true foundational moment in American political development."[92]

Other authors advanced APD into the twentieth century. *The United States as a Developing Country*, published in 1992, collected a set of essays by Martin Sklar that explained the development of "governmental structures" in the early twentieth century as a response to changes in the organization of American capitalism and the world economy.[93] Meanwhile Theda Skocpol's *Protecting Soldiers and Mothers*, also published in 1992, sought to explain the emergence of the American welfare state in the decades before World War II. Skocpol acknowledged the importance of changes such as industrialization and urbanization but resisted the argument that the emergence of a welfare state was a straightforward response to those changes. Like Skowrenek, Skocpol insisted that existing "institutional arrangements and political routines" played a critical role in determining how state structures evolved in response to changing social and economic conditions.[94]

By the mid-1990s, APD was a well-established subfield of American political science. It had its own journal, *Studies in American Political Development*, first published in 1986. And the American Political Science Association provided a home for APD in 1989, when it approved the establishment of its Politics and History Section, with a mandate to study, among other topics, the "developmental logic of institutions."[95] In 2003, APD was recognized as one of the most important modes of inquiry in American political science.[96] In 2004, the movement acquired its own "manifesto," *The Search for American Political Development*, by Karen Orren and Stephen Skowronek.[97]

The amount of scholarly work being done in APD by this time is too substantial to be neatly summarized. It included essay collections such as *Shaped by War and Trade*, edited by Ira Katznelson and Martin Shefter, which emphasized the relationship between "America's changing location in the international economy and state system and the development of its political institutions."[98] It also included monographs such as Brian Balogh's *A Government Out of Sight*, which challenged the conventional view that the American national government had a limited role in the nineteenth century. Balogh, like Leonard White, argued that the young nation's leaders were pragmatists, who responded vigorously to multiple challenges: "interstate rivalries, disorder on the frontiers, international threats to its security, competition for trade, and communications challenges."[99] But Balogh said the character of their response was determined by institutional and social constraints, which led to a preference for action through state and local governments, and voluntary and private groups, rather than by a national bureaucracy. The result was a state apparatus that governed as much as European nations, but less obviously. This argument was reprised by another APD scholar, Suzanne Mettler, in her widely discussed 2011 book, *The Submerged State*. Federal intervention in modern economic and social life is not less comprehensive than in other nations, Mettler argued, but it is much more difficult to see because it operates indirectly.[100]

Scholars in public administration who care about the subject of administrative development might look at this growing body of APD literature with a sense of regret. Not only is this work that they might have done; it is work that many pioneers in public administration insisted ought to be done within their field. But the initiative was taken instead by scholars in political science who had no real connection to the discipline of public administration. The attention that might have been drawn to scholars associated with public administration has been directed to other quarters. While public administration languishes, APD flourishes. A small indicator of this: the Politics and History Section of the APSA, home to APD scholars, organized twenty-one panel discussions at the association's 2013 meeting in Chicago—three times as many as the older Public Administration Section.

But it would be a mistake to assume that APD has eliminated the need for scholarship on administrative development, and the operation of large forces, within the discipline of public administration. There are several reasons why this is so. The first is that APD has a broader range of interests than scholars in public administration. Certainly many APD specialists have an interest in "administrative capacities," to borrow the phrase used by Skowronek in *Building a New American State*. In this respect there is a close connection to the interests of scholars in public administration. But APD is also interested in the "polity in all its different parts," as Orren and Skowronek observed in 2004.[101] This includes many subjects that may be of peripheral interest within the field of public administration, such as the evolution of legislatures, party systems, and nonstate actors that wield governing authority, such as churches or families.

So APD has broader ambitions. Paradoxically, though, it also suffers from a narrow conception of its methods. To understand how this is so, we should recall what large forces reasoning is about. The premise is that administrative development occurs because existing administrative structures prove inadequate for responding to challenges created by the operation of a set of large forces. Doctrine gives way to circumstances: as Woodrow Wilson said in 1885, government does what the times demand.

The APD literature is permeated with ambivalence about this premise. On one hand, many important works seem to recognize that large forces are important determinants of changes in state capacity. For example, Stephen Krasner observed in 1984 that the central issue in APD was "how institutional structures change in response to alterations in domestic and international environments."[102] On the other hand, and as we have noted, many writers in APD insist that the process of adaptation is not "rapid and fluid."[103] They are opposed to simplistic "functionalist" explanations of state development. The path and pace of adaptation, they insist, is determined by the character of political institutions that are in place at the time that new challenges arise.

As a general proposition, this is unobjectionable. The question is how much emphasis is to be put on existing state structures, rather than large forces, while crafting explanations about state development. Are large forces in the foreground while existing structures are in the background, or the reverse? On this question, APD made an early commitment that has been intensified over decades. In its determination to repudiate functionalism, APD insisted on the importance of existing structures. Large forces were gradually moved to the background of compositions in APD—sometimes so far back that they were barely visible.

In the inaugural issue of *Studies in American Political Development*, for example, Orren and Skowronek predicted that the journal would be a "proving ground for the claim that institutions have an independent and formative influence on politics."[104] In 2004, in *The Search for American Political Development*, Orren and Skowronek went further, saying that their main concern was "how changes in political institutions affect changes in the economy and society." Observe how the line of argument has been inverted in this second quotation. It is no longer a question of how existing structures mediate the effect of large forces. Rather, the proposition is now that state structures are themselves among the critical forces. They are, as Orren and Skowronek said, "prime movers" of development.[105] Other authors have made similar claims. Thus Theda Skocpol has argued that state agencies can be regarded as "sites of autonomous action" and that state officials often pursue policies "well ahead of social demands."[106]

Much of the APD literature is dedicated to validating this stance about the critical role of existing institutional arrangements in determining the path of state development. The central concern, in other words, is with the mechanisms of change, and only secondarily with the "exogenous shocks or shifts" that trigger those mechanisms.[107] This tendency to emphasize the role of existing institutions at the expense of large forces appears to have become more accentuated over time, perhaps because the subfield of APD is now institutionalized, and there are strong incentives for new scholars to refine concepts they have inherited from their teachers.

Given APD's emphasis on the tendency of institutions

to perpetuate themselves, this is a nice twist. And it also suggests an opportunity for scholars in public administration. No one can dispute the proposition that existing institutions will shape the way in which governments respond to the operation of large forces. Nor can we dispute that state actors sometimes act entrepreneurially, in anticipation of looming challenges. But all of this must be kept in perspective. Governments are powerful, but they do not dominate their environments. This is true even with regard to superpowers. Large forces act upon governments, and governments struggle to respond by overhauling their administrative capabilities. There is still plenty of room for scholars in public administration to explain how this occurs, and they can distinguish their work by giving more prominence to large forces than has been typical in the APD literature.

Moreover, it is possible for scholars in public administration to develop more sophisticated models of the processes by which large forces act upon governments. As we have noted, scholars in APD emphasize the role of existing institutions in mediating the effect of large forces. However, we can easily identify other factors that may play an equally important mediating role. Political culture or elite attitudes may also shape the response to large forces. So may the pattern in which interests are organized, or the presence of particularly talented leaders inside or outside government, or even chance events. Scholars in APD have attempted to stretch the institutionalist perspective to accommodate some of these other considerations. But there is no reason why scholars in public administration need to continue this effort. They can start from a relatively clean slate, developing forms of argument that give more prominence to large forces and accommodate a broader range of mediating factors.

5

WHY IT MATTERS

What's missing in the field of public administration? Two things: First, a recognition of the importance of research on the subject of administrative development, that is, the ways in which administrative systems develop over time. And second, a recognition of the relevance of large forces as variables in explaining the path of administrative development: why governments adopt and abandon functions, and why they use certain structures or techniques to execute those functions.

In short, we should work toward a broadened conception of what is contained within the domain of public administration scholarship. As we have seen, this broadened conception of the field is not new. On the contrary, it adheres closely to understandings that were prevalent within the field of public administration in its earliest years, and which were subsequently forgotten. So we are also arguing for a reappraisal of our current understanding of the intellectual history of public administration. We ought to abandon a simplistic and inaccurate narrative about prewar orthodoxy and replace it with a narrative that more accurately reflects how people in the field actually viewed the world around them at that time.

This call for a broadened conception of the domain of public administration should not be interpreted as a repudiation of the research already being done within it. There are many important questions within public administration that can be profitably explored without regard for large forces, and no one would suggest that sort of research should be abandoned. The argument here is only for recognizing the legitimacy of other research questions and new lines of analysis.

Nor should we confuse this call with a more general argument in favor of historical method in the field of public administration. Several scholars have argued that the field should pay more attention to history as a general matter, and this is undoubtedly right. But historical research can be oriented toward many different questions, some of which are, by the current standards of public administration scholarship, quite conventional. We could study public service motivation or red tape or network management in some earlier decade, and that would probably count as historical research. But if this research shows little regard for large forces as independent variables, then it is not the sort of research that is being called for here. It is simply a conventional form of research that is being pursued with older data. The sort of historical research that *would* be germane is oriented to larger questions of administrative development, and concerned with exploring the evolution of functions and techniques in relation to the operation of large forces.

Indeed, it is possible to undertake the sort of analysis that is being called for here without undertaking historical research at all—assuming that, by calling research historical, we mean only that the materials that are used are older than the researcher.[108] It is entirely possible to ask big questions about administrative development—and the operation of large forces—with regard to recent events. If Leonard White had not died in 1958, he might have finished a fifth volume of his series that extended into the New Deal, which was a period of which he had firsthand knowledge. Indeed, he had already supervised doctoral dissertations that examined administrative development under three twentieth-century presidents: Taft, Wilson, and Hoover.[109] White's protégé J. E. Hodgetts published a study in 1973 of the Canadian public service that ended in 1970—which is to say, only a few months before its publication. All of which is to repeat the point: what matters is the questions that are asked, and the kinds of answers that are advanced, not the period of time to which the study pertains.

Why should we revive the mode of analysis that I have called large forces reasoning? One way to answer this question would be to pose another one. We have seen that authors and editors of critical texts sometimes provide this sort of analysis, albeit in an informal and undisciplined way. They undertaken this analysis even though, according their own definitions of the boundaries of the field, it is not the sort of thing that scholars in public administration ought to be doing. Then why do they do it? Earlier I suggested that authors and editors might be driven by the needs of readers, and especially of readers who are new to the field, who are not yet blinded by doctrine about the boundaries of inquiry, and who therefore ask the perfectly reasonable question: How did this vast apparatus of government come to acquire its present scale and design?

Large forces scholarship can help us to produce rigorous, persuasive answers to this question. It will provide scholars in the field with a richer understanding of how the administrative apparatus of government acquired its present form. Large forces scholarship can also help us draw on the past to understand how the process of adaptation to large forces will proceed in the future. For example, we have given considerable attention recently to the ways in which new information technologies are affecting public administration. But we have tended to treat this as a *sui generis* phenomenon, rather than as one instance drawn from the larger category of technological innovations that have affected American government over the last two centuries. Our capacity to understand this particular period of innovation would be improved if we had a better understanding of earlier periods.[110] A similar argument can be made with regard to other large forces. Over the past two centuries, American government has responded to multiple shifts in the structure of international relations, in the structure of domestic and international economic activity, and in demography, and to multiple new threats to public health. We ought to be able to draw on these experiences to provide intelligent advice about how future adaptations can be managed well. The method by which we do this is straightforward: we need to produce well-researched articles and books that carefully trace the process by which particular forces induce change in administrative structures.[111]

The revival of large forces reasoning may also serve another purpose: it may help to reverse the long-term decline in public perceptions about the importance of public administration scholarship. Evidence about the decline in public attention to scholarly work in public administration is all around us. We saw some of this evidence earlier, in our discussion of *Fear Itself*. Books by political scientists, economists, historians, and sociologists are regularly noted in the journals that provide advice to the retail bookselling trade. Books by scholars in public administration are rarely, if ever, regarded as noteworthy.

Another way to gauge the decline of public administration since its founding is by contrasting media coverage of the field sixty years ago and now. For instance, in 1950, any regular reader of the *New York Times*, a major media outlet, would have recognized that public administration was one of the most dynamic fields of scholarly inquiry in the United States. The term "public administration" appeared in the newspaper 102 times that year. About a dozen of these appearances were in advertisements, obituaries, and marriage announcements. But there were still dozens of stories that told about the work of scholars in public administration. The pages of the *New York Times* showed that policymakers and citizens were looking to the field for advice on how to manage wrenching changes in domestic and global affairs.

What was the news about public administration in the *New York Times* in 1950? Among other things, that Luther Gulick had been approached "to make a survey of the whole government of New York City," which had grown by over two million people in the preceding three decades.[112] That public administration experts at the University of California were helping West Coast ports "regain world trade."[113] That Donald Price of the Public Administration Clearing House had been recruited to guide a study on "the functioning of the United States Government in world affairs."[114] That Herbert Simon had published an important new book examining "the operation of government, from the taxpayer's point of view."[115] That Edward Litchfield, a professor of public administration at Cornell University, was urging "forthright action" to avert crisis in occupied Germany.[116] That Roscoe Martin, former president of the American Society of Public Administration, was worried about the rising influence of single-interest lobbies.[117] That Stuart Symington, appointed by Truman to undertake economic planning for the Cold War, was the sort of person "of whom, public administration students tell us, the country stands in dire need."[118] And that other public administration specialists were advising the federal government on the reform of policies on education and agriculture. In short, a reader of the *New York Times* in 1950 would have been impressed by the extent to which leaders in the field were setting the terms of debate on a host of critical issues.

Now move the clock forward fifty years. In 2000, there were only sixty-four references to the phrase "public administration" in the *New York Times*—forty fewer than in 1950. Furthermore, hardly any of those references described a substantive contribution by scholars in public administration to debates about domestic or global affairs. Forty were in advertisements for MPA programs, and fourteen were marriage announcements for newly minted MPA graduates or obituaries for retired faculty and public servants. Of the remaining ten articles, some simply used the phrase to describe the bureaucracy of other nations.

This transformation in coverage was peculiar to public administration. For example, from 1950 to 2000, the number of references in the *New York Times* to political science did not decline. (There were 236 references in 1950, and 248 in 2000.) And in 2000, only 20 percent of these references were found in advertisements, marriage announcements, or obituaries—as opposed to 83 percent of the references to public administration.[119] The newspaper's reportage on public administration in 2000 revealed a field that was more professionalized, but also less engaged in public affairs.

Indeed, the shift in the relative status of public administration and political science since the 1930s has been extraordinary. Consider the individuals who served as presidents of the American Political Science Association at that time. Clarence Dykstra, APSA president in 1937–38, was a former city manager. Robert Cushman, president in 1942-43, had worked on the research staff of the President's Committee on Administrative Management. Cushman was followed by Leonard White, who was elected APSA president in 1943 while he was still editor of *Public Administration Review*. White was followed by John Gaus. (Gaus used his presidential address to make another appeal for an ecological approach to scholarship. "Our job," he said, is to explain "the significance of physical, social, and intellectual change upon government as an instrument by means of which people first may live at all, and live better."[120]) Arthur Macmahon, president in 1946-47, was another veteran of the President's Committee. And Luther Gulick served as APSA president in 1950-51.

Times have changed. It has been years since a prominent scholar in public administration has served as APSA president (although two leaders in APD have filled that role: Ira Katznelson in 2005-6, and Theda Skocpol in 2002-3). The fall of public administration is further illustrated by a letter written by APSA president Jane Mansbridge in March 2013. Mansbridge, a professor at Harvard University's Kennedy School of Government, told federal legislators that political science "is the *only* discipline devoted to learning how to make democracies work better."[121] This might be a defensible statement if public administration is construed as a subfield of political science rather than its own discipline. But the *Public Administration Theory Primer* assures us that public administration is its own discipline. So does *Classics of Public Administration*.[122] Either the *Primer* and *Classics* are wrong, or Mansbridge does not think much of the discipline of public administration.

What has caused the decline in attention to scholarship in public administration, either by the public at large, or by scholars in related fields? It might be tempting to argue that "questions of governmental function and arrangement," as Edward Corwin once called them, are less important today than they were in the 1930s and 1940s, and that consequently there is less interest in what scholars in public administration have to say about those questions.[123] But as we think over the crises of the last decade—such as terrorism, financial collapse, climate change, mass migrations, and pandemics—we realize that this argument cannot be right. The costs of administrative failure are just as high today as they were seventy and eighty years ago.[124]

A more plausible argument is that the field of public administration has been weakened because of a shift in attitude about the boundaries for research within the field. Scholars in public administration have steadily retreated from conversation about big questions of governance. We have chosen not to tell well-developed stories about the ways in which governments have grappled with major challenges, and we do not write so that our arguments are appealing to a broad audience. Instead, we have dwelt excessively on problems of administrative technique, with the hope that these will be more tractable. But these small problems sometimes prove to be equally intractable and, for a wider audience, largely uninteresting.

There is a way to revive interest in the field of public administration, which involves approaching the field just as many academics did in the 1930s and 1940s. It should be clear by now that this does not mean formulating desiccated principles of administration. On the contrary, it means expanding the boundaries of the field so that we recognize the legitimacy of research on the overall development of the administrative apparatus of government. It also means recognizing the extent to which large forces influence the path of administrative development. And it involves an exploration of the way in which institutions and other factors influence the process of administrative adaptation to the operation of large forces. This sort of research will help scholars in the field understand where public administration has been, and where it is going. This type of research, elegantly done, will attract the public attention that the field once took for granted.

NOTES

Epigraph: Adapted from W.R.S. Ralston, ed., *Krilof and His Fables* (London: Strahan and Company, 1871), 43.

[1] Woodrow Wilson, *The State* (Boston: D. C. Heath, 1889), 651.

[2] Tina Nabatchi, "The (Re)Discovery of the Public in Public Administration," *Public Administration Review* 70 (2010): s309.

[3] Henry A. Turner, "Woodrow Wilson: Exponent of Executive Leadership," *Western Political Quarterly* 4, no. 1 (1951): 114. See also Henry A. Turner, "Woodrow Wilson as Administrator," *Public Administration Review* 16, no. 4 (1956): 257.

[4] Dwight Waldo also talked about a prewar orthodoxy in his 1948 book *The Administrative State*. But Waldo used the term more cautiously. The word was always presented in scare quotes and Waldo repeatedly acknowledged that there was "a considerable measure of doubt and even iconoclasm" in the field even during the supposed heyday of orthodox thinking. Dwight Waldo, *The Administrative State: A Study of the Political Theory of American Public Administration* (New York: Ronald Press, 1948), 75, 206, 211. Sayre removed these caveats and introduced the hard-edged conception of orthodoxy that prevails today.

[5] Wallace S. Sayre, "Premises of Public Administration: Past and Emerging," *Public Administration Review* 18, no. 2 (1958): 103-104.

[6] Beryl A. Radin, "Reclaiming Our Past: Linking Theory and Practice." *PS: Political Science & Politics* 46, no. 1 (2013): 4-5.

[7] Donald Worster, *Dust Bowl: The Southern Plains in the 1930s* (New York: Oxford University Press, 1979), 12.

[8] Charles E. Merriam, "Progress in Political Research," *American Political Science Review* 20, no. 1 (1926): 6.

NOTES

[9] Charles E. Merriam, *Political Power: Its Composition and Incidence* (New York: McGraw-Hill, 1934), 325-326.

[10] Leonard D. White, *The Future of Government in the United States* (Chicago: University of Chicago Press, 1942).

[11] Luther H. Gulick, Lyndall F. Urwick, and Carl H. Pforzheimer, *Papers on the Science of Administration* (New York: Institute of Public Administration, 1937).

[12] The phrases are drawn from Luther H. Gulick, *American Forest Policy* (New York: Deull, Sloan and Pearce, 1951), 55; and Luther H. Gulick, *Administrative Reflections from World War II* (University, AL: University of Alabama Press, 1948), 31.

[13] Luther H. Gulick, "Reflections on Public Administration, Past and Present," *Public Administration Review* 50, no. 6 (1990): 602. See also Luther H. Gulick, "Democracy and Administration Face the Future," *Public Administration Review* 37, no. 6 (1977): 707.

[14] Luther H. Gulick, "Politics, Administration, and the 'New Deal,'" *Annals of the American Academy of Political and Social Science* 169 (1933): 63.

[15] Gulick, *Administrative Reflections*, 1. Emphasis added.

[16] Gulick, *American Forest Policy*, 63.

[17] Ibid., 12-13.

[18] John M. Gaus, "Review of *American Forest Policy*," *Journal of Politics* 14, no. 4 (1952): 738-739.

[19] John M. Gaus, "The Present Status of the Study of Public Administration in the United States," *American Political Science Review* 25, no. 1 (1931): 121-123.

[20] John M. Gaus, Leon O. Wolcott, and Verne B. Lewis, *Public Administration and the United States Department of Agriculture* (Chicago: Public Administration Service, 1940), 35, 58, 115.

[21] Ibid., 378, 380.

[22] John M. Gaus, *Reflections on Public Administration* (University, AL: University of Alabama Press, 1947), 1-19.

[23] John M. Gaus, "The Mingling of Study and Practice in Public Administration," *Western Political Quarterly* 4, no. 4 (1951): 625-626, 629.

[24] Earle D. Ross, "The Civil War Agricultural New Deal," *Social Forces* 15, no. 1 (1936): 97-104.

[25] Gaus, Wolcott, and Lewis, *Public Administration*, 7.

[26] Carl F. Taeusch, "A Symposium on Administration," *Public Administration Review* 1, no. 2 (1941): 211.

[27] Schuyler C. Wallace, *Federal Departmentalization: A Critique of Theories of Organization* (New York: Columbia University Press, 1941), 232-233.

[28] Louis Smith, "Alexis De Tocqueville and Public Administration," *Public Administration Review* 2, no. 3 (1942): 236.

[29] The two articles are Lynton K. Caldwell, "Thomas Jefferson and Public Administration," *Public Administration Review* 3, no. 3 (1943): 240-253; Lynton K. Caldwell, "Alexander Hamilton: Advocate of Executive Leadership," *Public Administration Review* 4, no. 2 (1944): 113-126. The quotation is drawn from Lynton K. Caldwell, "Novus Ordo Seclorum: The Heritage of American Public Administration," *Public Administration Review* 36, no. 5 (1976): 476.

[30] Lynton K. Caldwell, "The Relevance of Administrative History," *International Review of Administrative Sciences* 21, no. 3 (1955): 461.

[31] David M. Levitan, "Political Ends and Administrative Means," *Public Administration Review* 3, no. 4 (1943): 354; Don K. Price, "A Response to Mr. Laski," *Public Administration Review* 4, no. 4 (1944): 360; Vincent M. Barnett Jr., "Modern Constitutional Development: A Challenge to Administration," *Public Administration Review* 4, no. 2 (1944): 159.

NOTES

[32] J. Donald Kingsley, "Political Ends and Administrative Means: The Administrative Principles of Hamilton and Jefferson," *Public Administration Review* 5, no. 1 (1945): 89.

[33] Robert A. Dahl, "The Science of Public Administration: Three Problems," *Public Administration Review* 7, no. 1 (1947): 8, 11. Emphasis in original.

[34] Laurence E. Lynn, "Restoring the Rule of Law to Public Administration: What Frank Goodnow Got Right and Leonard White Didn't," *Public Administration Review* 69, no. 5 (2009): 803-813.

[35] Quoted in: Levitan, "Political Ends," 355.

[36] Herbert Storing, "Leonard D. White and the Study of Public Administration," *Public Administration Review* 25, no. 1 (1965): 46-47.

[37] Ibid., 45.

[38] Harvey Mansfield, "Review of *The Republican Era*," *Public Administration Review* 19, no. 3 (1959): 186.

[39] Dumas Malone, "Before Patronage Took Over," *New York Times*, October 21, 1951, 197.

[40] Dumas Malone, "Democracy in Power," *New York Times*, September 19, 1954, BR22.

[41] Richard R. John, "Leonard D. White and the Invention of American Administrative History," *Reviews in American History* 24, no. 2 (1996): 352.

[42] The following discussion draws on Alasdair Roberts, "The Path Not Taken: Leonard White and the Macrodynamics of Administrative Development." *Public Administration Review* 69, no. 4 (2009): 764-775.

[43] Leonard D. White, *The Republican Era, 1869-1901: A Study in Administrative History* (New York: Macmillan, 1958), 1.

44 Leonard D. White, *The Jeffersonians: A Study in Administrative History, 1801-1829* (New York: Macmillan, 1951), 5, 131, 432.

45 Leonard D. White, *The Jacksonians: A Study in Administrative History, 1829-1861* (New York: Macmillan, 1954), 7, 48.

46 David M. Potter, "Book Review: *The Federalists, the Jeffersonians*," *William and Mary Quarterly* 9, no. 2 (1952): 269.

47 Charles Wiltse, "Some Reflections on Administrative History," *Public Administration Review* 12, no. 2 (1952): 113.

48 John M. Gaus, "Review of *The Federalists*," *Public Administration Review* 8, no. 4 (1948): 290.

49 Lucius Wilmerding Jr., "Some Notes on Administrative History," *Public Administration Review* 15, no. 2 (1955): 102.

50 Paul P. Van Riper, *History of the United States Civil Service* (Evanston, IL: Row, Peterson, 1958), xiii-xiv. Van Riper observes that the "foundation for this study was laid even before World War II," under the guidance of Leonard White.

51 J. E. Hodgetts, *Pioneer Public Service* (Toronto: University of Toronto Press, 1955).

52 J. E. Hodgetts, "Challenge and Response: A Retrospective View of the Public Service of Canada," *Canadian Public Administration* 7, no. 4 (1964): 409.

53 John M. Gaus, "Review of *Pioneer Public Service*," *American Political Science Review* 51, no. 1 (1957): 235.

54 J. E. Hodgetts, *The Canadian Public Service: A Physiology of Government, 1867-1970* (Toronto: University of Toronto Press, 1973), 17; J. I. Gow et al., "The Intellectual Legacy of J. E. Hodgetts," *Canadian Public Administration* 54, no. 2 (2011): 167.

55 H. George Frederickson et al., *The Public Administration Theory Primer*, 2nd ed. (Boulder, CO: Westview Press, 2012).

56 Ibid., Kindle location 84.

57 Ibid., Kindle location 2163, 3068, 3515, 4563, 4645.

NOTES

58 Ibid., Kindle location 159.

59 Ibid., Kindle location 5200.

60 From the Cengage Learning webpage for the seventh edition, http://tinyurl.com/lrtj4p7. The endorsement is provided by Professor John Kiefer of the University of New Orleans.

61 Jay M. Shafritz and Albert C. Hyde, *Classics of Public Administration*, 7th ed. (Boston: Wadsworth/Cengage Learning, 2012), back cover.

62 Shafritz and Hyde, *Classics of Public Administration*, 11, 67, 75.

63 Ibid., 12, 53-54.

64 Ibid., xi.

65 Ibid.

66 Ibid., xii, 4, 11, 67, 77, 171, 371.

67 David H. Rosenbloom, Robert Kravchuck, and Richard M. Clerkin, *Public Administration: Understanding Management, Politics, and Law in the Public Sector*, 7th ed. (Boston: McGraw-Hill, 2009).

68 Jane Beckett-Camarata and Larkin Dudley, "Educating American Public Administrators: Texts for the Introductory Course," *Public Administration Review* 70, no. 4 (2010): 634.

69 Rosenbloom, Kravchuck, and Clerkin, *Public Administration*,, 3, 5, 14.

70 Ibid., 14-15.

71 Ibid., 43.

72 Ibid., 3, 14, 15.

73 Ibid., 47-49. I have omitted one paragraph that identifies certain federal agencies as "clientele departments," and defines that concept.

74 Ibid., 470.

75 Ibid., 186.

76 Ibid., 256-258, 283, 335.

77 Ibid., 204.

78 Ibid., 385.

79 Ibid., 395.

80 Donald A. Schon, *The Reflective Practitioner: How Professionals Think in Action* (New York: Basic Books, 1983).

81 *Kirkus Reviews*, December 1, 2012.

82 *Publishers Weekly*, December 17, 2012, 49-50.

83 2013 Leonard White Lecture, University of Chicago, http://vimeo.com/65033477.

84 Karen Orren and Stephen Skowronek, *The Search for American Political Development* (New York: Cambridge University Press, 2004), 1.

85 John Gerring, "APD from a Methodological Point of View," *Studies in American Political Development* 17, no. 01 (2003): 86.

86 Stephen Skowronek, *Building a New American State* (New York: Cambridge University Press, 1982), viii-ix, 4.

87 Stephen D. Krasner, "Approaches to the State: Alternative Conceptions and Historical Dynamics," *Comparative Politics* 16, no. 2 (1984): 238.

88 Gulick, *Administrative Reflections*, 1. Emphasis added.

89 Richard A. Brisbin Jr., "The Transformation of the American State," *Review of Politics* 45, no. 2 (1983): 319.

90 Orren and Skowronek, *Search for American Political Development*, 2.

91 Richard F. Bensel, *Sectionalism and American Political Development, 1880-1980* (Madison: University of Wisconsin Press, 1984), xix.

NOTES

[92] Richard F. Bensel, *Yankee Leviathan: The Origins of Central State Authority in America, 1859-1877* (New York: Cambridge University Press, 1990), ix-x, 10.

[93] Martin J. Sklar, *The United States as a Developing Country: Studies in U.S. History in the Progressive Era and the 1920s* (New York: Cambridge University Press, 1992).

[94] Theda Skocpol, *Protecting Soldiers and Mothers: The Political Origins of Social Policy in the United States* (Cambridge: Belknap Press of Harvard University Press, 1992), 14, 40, 66.

[95] APSA Politics and History Section, by-laws, as revised Spring 2008.

[96] Ira Katznelson and Helen V. Milner, *Political Science: State of the Discipline* (New York: W. W. Norton, 2002), 722-754.

[97] Orren and Skowronek, *Search for American Political Development*. The description is provided by Ronald J. Pestritto, "Politics and History," *The Review of Politics* 67, no. 3 (2005): 580.

[98] Ira Katznelson and Martin Shefter, *Shaped by War and Trade: International Influences on American Political Development* (Princeton: Princeton University Press, 2002), ix.

[99] Brian Balogh, *A Government Out of Sight: The Mystery of National Authority in Nineteenth-Century America* (New York: Cambridge University Press, 2009), 10.

[100] Suzanne Mettler, *The Submerged State: How Invisible Government Policies Undermine American Democracy* (Chicago: University of Chicago Press, 2011).

[101] Orren and Skowronek, *Search for American Political Development*, 1.

[102] Krasner, "Approaches to the State," 224.

[103] Ibid., 234.

[104] Karen Orren and Stephen Skowronek, editors' preface, *Studies in American Political Development* 1, no. 1 (1986): vii.

[105] Orren and Skowronek, *Search for American Political Development*, 80, 91-95.

[106] Skocpol, *Protecting Soldiers and Mothers*, 42.

[107] James Mahoney and Kathleen Ann Thelen, eds., *Explaining Institutional Change: Ambiguity, Agency, and Power* (New York: Cambridge University Press, 2010), 6.

[108] For a more refined definition, see Jos C. N. Raadschelders, *Handbook of Administrative History* (New Brunswick, NJ: Transaction Publishers, 1998), 6-8.

[109] The dissertations were completed by Henry A. Turner (1950), John L. Withers (1956), and John L. Westrate (1963).

[110] The effect of technological change is discussed by Christopher Pollitt in *New Perspectives on Public Services: Place and Technology* (New York: Oxford University Press, 2002). There is a tendency in this study, however, to narrow the focus to recent changes in information technologies.

[111] For a further comment on appropriate methods, see Robert Durant, "Parsimony, "Error" Terms, and the Future of a Field." *Public Administration Review* 70 (2010): s319-s320.

[112] "A City Government Survey," *New York Times*, January 7, 1950, 11.

[113] "Sea Trade Sought by San Francisco," *New York Times*, May 29, 1950, 20.

[114] "Foundation Plans U.S. Policy Study," *New York Times*, September 11, 1950, 14.

[115] "Books of the Week," *New York Times*, September 10, 1950, 222.

[116] Edward H. Litchfield, "The Hour of Crisis Nears in Germany," *New York Times*, May 14, 1950, 187.

[117] Warren Weaver Jr., "U.S. Found Moving into City Affairs," *New York Times*, November 21, 1950, 33.

NOTES

[118] Cabell Phillips, "Key Man of Our Mobilization," *New York Times*, October 10, 1950, 177.

[119] To anticipate another response: The coverage of political science was not artificially boosted by the presidential election in 2000. The same trends are evident if we compare 1949 to 1999 or 1951 to 2001.

[120] John M. Gaus, "A Job Analysis of Political Science," *American Political Science Review* 40, no. 2 (1946): 226.

[121] Jane Mansbridge and Michael Brintnall, *Letter to Congress Regarding Funding by the National Science Foundation* (Washington, DC: American Political Science Association, March 15, 2013). Emphasis added.

[122] There are repeated references to the discipline of public administration throughout both texts. For example: *Public Administration Theory Primer*, Kindle location 893, 944, 967, 994, 1163; *Classics of Public Administration*, ix, xi.

[123] Edward Corwin, "Social Planning under the Constitution," *American Political Science Review* 26, no. 1 (1932): 27.

[124] A similar point is made by Robert Durant in "Whither the Neoadministrative State? Toward a Polity-Centered Theory of Administrative Reform." *Journal of Public Administration Research and Theory* 10, no. 4 (2000): 104.

Made in the USA
Monee, IL
24 July 2020